Mapwork

1

WRITTEN BY
David Flint
AND
Mandy Suhr

ILLUSTRATED BY
Damon Burnard

Books in the series

Mapwork 1
Mapwork 2

First published in 1992 by
Wayland (Publishers) Limited
61 Western Road, Hove
East Sussex, BN3 1JD, England

**British Library Cataloguing in
Publication Data**

**Flint, David
Mapwork 1
1. Title 11. Suhr, Mandy
372.89**

PAPERBACK ISBN 0-7502-0515-6

**Editor: Mandy Suhr
Consultant: Julie Warne**

Designed by Helter Skelter
Typeset by Matt Black dtp
Printed in Italy by G.Canale and C.S.p.A., Turin

Contents

Words that appear in **bold** are explained in the glossary.

Fairy-tale forest

Little Red Riding Hood is going to visit her granny in fairy-tale forest. This **map** shows her **route**.

How many houses does she pass?

Can you guess who lives in each house?

Make your own model of fairy-tale forest from plasticine. Draw a map of your forest.

This is the maze
in the castle gardens.
Cinderella has
lost her crown.

Can you help her to find it?

5

Where's the wolf?

The wolf has followed Red Riding Hood. Here are some of his hiding places. Can you spot him...

behind a tree...

above, in a tree...

in front of a gate...

outside granny's cottage...

inside the Three Bears' house...

below the bridge?

Make a poster of **direction** words for your classroom.

Play this game. Follow the directions to see who can get to the castle first. You will need a dice and markers for players.

Looking from above

Look at these photographs of different toys.

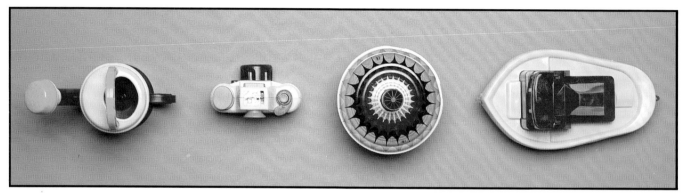

This is how they look from above.

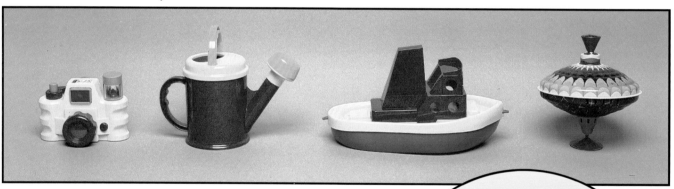

This is how they look from the side.

Can you match the toys in the two photographs?

Choose five objects from your classroom. Draw what they look like from above. Can your friend match the drawings to the objects?

Here is a **plan** of a table. A plan is a view from above. The children have drawn around each object to show what it would look like from above.

Look carefully at the photograph. Can you spot anything that they have missed?

Making maps

These children have made a model of their street from cardboard boxes. They are drawing a map to go with it. Can you help them?

Make a model of your street with some friends. Can you make a map of your model street?

Copy this street plan. Draw in the model buildings as they look from above.

A bird's-eye view

This photograph was taken from an aeroplane high in the sky.
It is called an **aerial photograph**.

Look carefully, what can you see?

Look for the boats on the river.

Look for the cars on the road.

Can you see the swimming pool?

Look at the buildings. Some are bigger than others.
What do you think they might be?

Can you see any people?
Why do you think they are so difficult to see?

Q: What is this?

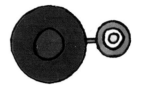

A: A man wearing a big hat and frying an egg in a pan.

With your friends, make a list of all the things you can see in this photograph.
Who can spot the most things?

13

Follow a route

Class 4 are visiting the safari park. This is the route that they follow to get to the lake. Can you follow it on the map?

Straight on past the elephants and the zebras.
Turn right.
Turn left.
Straight on again.

Plan a route from the lions to the adventure playground.

Plan a route from the playground to the monkeys.

14

Plan a route around your school for a friend to follow. Can they follow your directions?

Compass directions

We can use a **compass** to help us find exact directions. The four main directions are NORTH, SOUTH, EAST and WEST.

To find where they are, turn the compass around until the needle points to N for North. Then you will be able to see where East, West and South are to be found.

Make your own signpost map.

Kathy and her friends have drawn a signpost map. It shows some of the things they can see in their classroom.

- What can they see to the East?
- What can they see to the North?
- What can they see to the South?
- What can they see to the West?

17

Using a grid

We use a **grid** to help us find things on a map.
Each **column** has a letter.
Each **row** has a number.

To find the letter of a square, move your finger down the column to the bottom of the grid.
To find the number of a square, move your finger across the row to the side of the grid.

The circle on this grid is at B3.
The diamond is at D2.

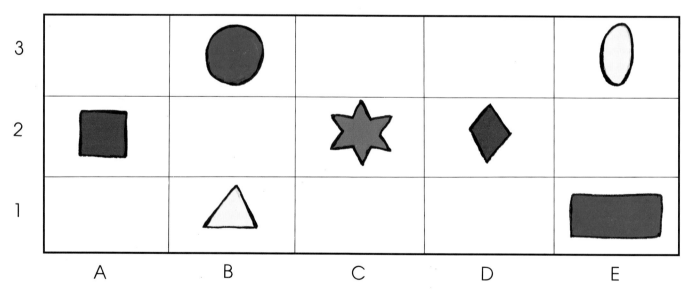

Where can you find...
- a star?   • a triangle?   • a square?
- a rectangle?   • an oval?

Where on this grid can you find...

- a fish?
- a ball?
- a crown?
- a fly?
- a hat?
- a chair?
- a dog?
- a watch?
- a television?
- a cat?

Finding the right place

Gruesome Gertie has a new assistant, Maisie. She is going to help Gertie make her spells and potions. Gertie has labelled her shelves to help Maisie find the right ingredients.

fish scales
dragon's bogies
spider's legs
skeleton bones
fingernails
dried slugs
bat's wings
frog's toes
snail slime
beetle's brains
2
1
A
B
C
D
E

Each shelf now has a letter and a number.

The letter shows which column the shelf is in. The number shows which row the shelf is in.

The spider's legs are in C2. The dried slugs are in A1.

Where will Maisie find the things on Gertie's list?

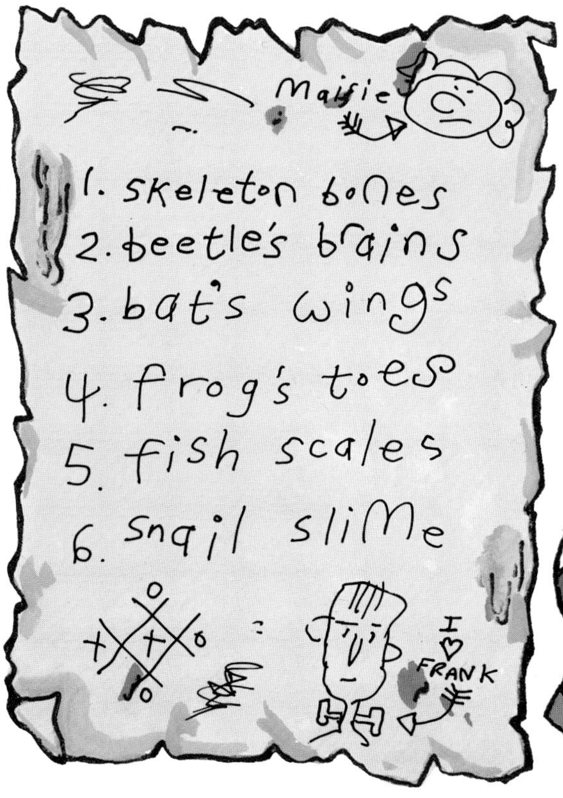
Maisie
1. skeleton bones
2. beetle's brains
3. bat's wings
4. frog's toes
5. fish scales
6. snail slime
I ♡ FRANK

Treasure island

This map was found in a bottle. The note
was written by One-Eyed Jake the pirate.
It shows where he buried
his treasure.

Follow Jake's instructions to find which square the treasure is buried in.

My ship sank in Shark Bay (B7). I swam to the island. I set off to look for a good place to bury my treasure. I came to a swamp. It was very smelly so I didn't bury it there (E7). I came to a tall mountain. It was very cold so I didn't bury it there (J7). I came to a dark forest. It was full of giant spiders, so I didn't bury it there (I4). I came to a river. I swam across. It was very muddy so I didn't bury it there (I2). I came to a cave near a sandy beach. There were lots of crocodiles to guard it. I did bury it there (A5). One-Eyed Jake

Make your own treasure map. Write some **instructions** to lead to your treasure. Can a friend guess where your treasure is buried?

23

If you had some treasure where would you bury it?

Signs around us

We can see **signs** all around us. They give us lots of different kinds of information.

Some signs give a warning.

No cycling

Some signs tell us about things we must not do.

Some signs give directions.

Playground

Some signs tell us where we can find things.

These are some signs from around the world.
Can you guess what they mean?

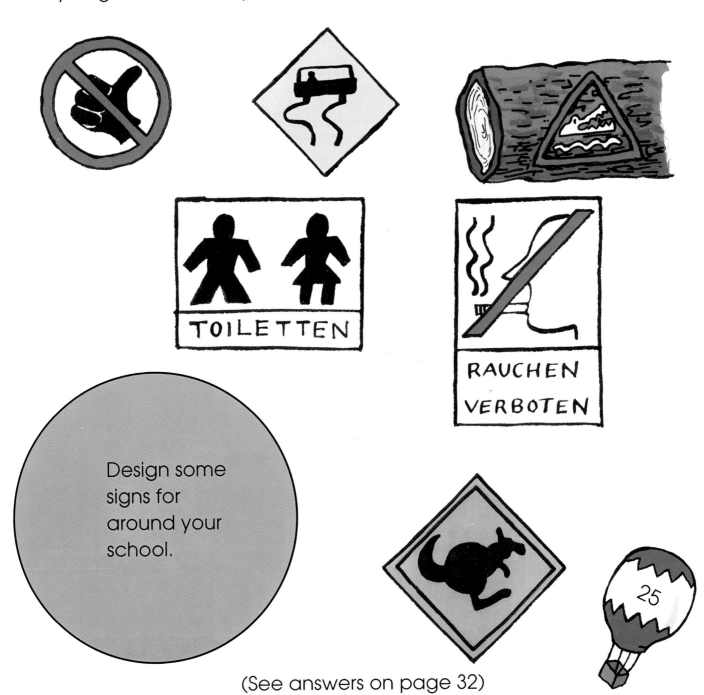

TOILETTEN

RAUCHEN VERBOTEN

Design some signs for around your school.

25

(See answers on page 32)

Cracking the code

Symbols are used on maps. They are special kinds of signs.
They show you where to find things.
These two maps both show the same place.
The second map uses symbols instead of drawings.

26

Can you tell what each symbol means?
Look at this **key** to help you.
A key shows the reader what each symbol means.

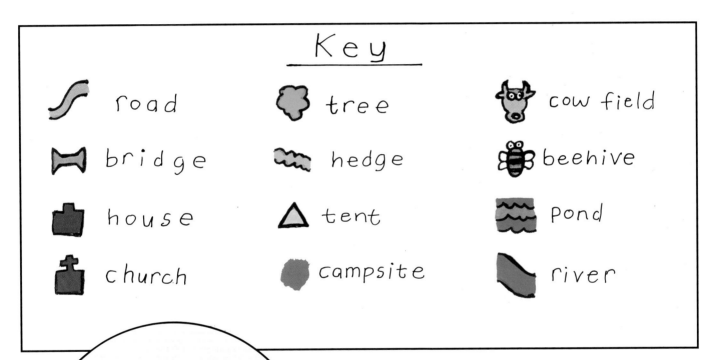

Key

road	tree	cow field
bridge	hedge	beehive
house	tent	pond
church	campsite	river

Make an imaginary map. Design symbols for the things on your map. Make a key to show what the symbols mean.

Design some symbols of your own. How would you show...

• a jungle?
• a zoo?
• a restaurant?

• a shipwreck?
• a school?

27

Holiday time

Joe and Katie are going to visit Adventureland.
There are lots of things for them to do and see.
This map will help them to find their way around.

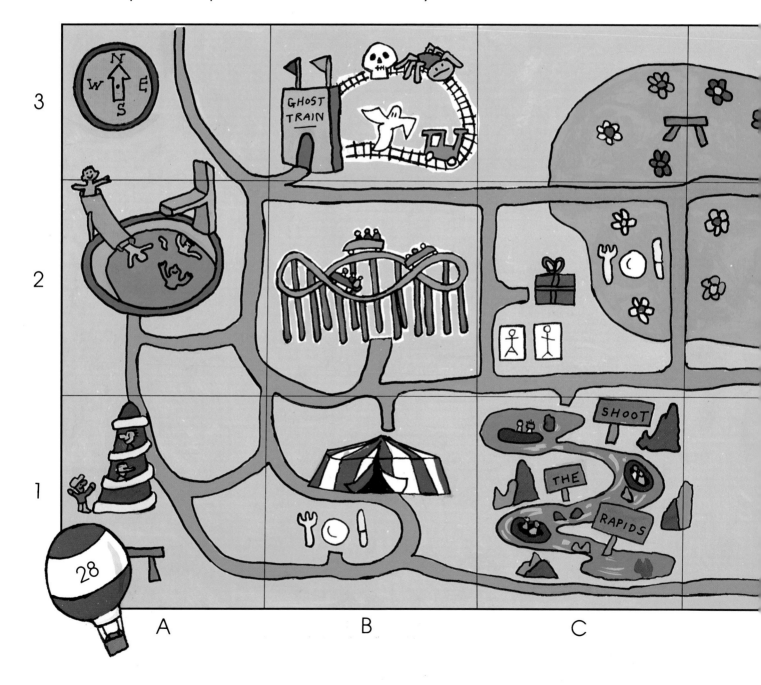

If you were to visit Adventureland, what would you like to do?
Choose five things and describe the route that you would
follow to get to them.

E

Use the grid to help you.

Where would
you find the toilets?

Where could
you eat lunch?

Where could you
buy souvenirs?

Make your own map
of an imaginary place.

Key

🍴⊙🍴 café

Picnic area

🎁 gift shop

⛺ Big Top

🍦 ice cream stall

🧍🧍 toilets

🌸 Park

Glossary

Aerial photograph A photograph taken from high up in the sky, usually from an aeroplane or a balloon.

Column A line running from top to bottom.

Compass A tool used to measure direction.

Direction The way that you face when you want to travel somewhere.

Grid A pattern of numbered squares printed on a map, arranged in columns and rows. The grid helps you to find things quickly.

Instructions Ways of telling someone how to do something.

Key The part of a map that tells you what each symbol means.

Map An accurate drawing that shows the shape of a place, and the things that are there.

Plan A map of a building, street or town as it looks from above.

Route The path that you decide to travel when you want to go somewhere.

Row A line running from side to side.

Sign A mark or a symbol that has a special meaning.

Symbol A shape or a small picture that helps you to find something quickly on a map.

Books to read

Moving Into Maps (Heinemann Educational, 1984)
Going Places: Mapping Skills (Thomas Nelson and Sons, 1987)
Mapstart 1 by Simon Catling (Collins.Longman, 1985)
Keystart First Atlas (Collins.Longman, 1991)
First Picture Atlas (Wayland, 1992)

Notes for adults

Map reading is one of the most important geographical skills that children need to develop. This book can be used in school or at home and has been designed to enable young children to acquire this skill quickly and painlessly.

The book consists of a series of fun activities and games, which build a framework of skills and concepts necessary for map interpretation. There are also ideas for extension work with each activity.

The use of maps is the principal focus of the National Geography Curriculum: Attainment Target 1. MAPWORK 1 meets the requirements of Key Stage 1, levels 1–3.

Pupils at Key Stage 1 should be able to:–

- follow directions using terms such as up, down, front, left, right, etc.
- talk about what is shown on a pictorial map
- talk about places familiar or unfamiliar
- draw around objects to make a plan
- follow a route on a plan
- identify land and sea on maps and globes
- use four compass points: North, South, East and West
- identify features on an aerial photograph
- use letter and number co-ordinates to locate features on a map
- extract information from large scale maps.

This book explores all of these skills.

Index

Acknowledgements
Photographs supplied by:
Geonex U.K. 12; Helter Skelter (Paul Mattock) 8,9,10.

The publishers would also like to thank Patcham Infant School
for their kind co-operation.

Answers from page 25.
From top left: No hitch-hiking (U.S.A.), Slippery roads (U.S.A.),
Beware of crocodiles (Australia), Toilets (Germany),
No smoking (Germany), Kangaroos ahead (Australia).